An excellent autobiography of Jan's psychological journey of personal insight, acceptance, and healing from the past and folding it into the present. Her story is a therapeutic description of how powerful understanding all parts of our self can be in making good life choices. This book will strike a chord with any reader.

– Deb Schierbeck, LCPC

Reading this book is like opening a window to the soul, one that may have been muddling through each day, unaware that the truth of our adult existence lies within our past experiences. This author has brought to light the powerful message that by communicating with our inner child, by loving our past selves, by protecting and cherishing that child that we all keep hidden within, we can become the person we were put on this earth to be. We can be free, happy, and fulfilled. By reading this book, I came to understand that my inner child (which I had not realized existed) was crying out to be heard and loved and healed. As the author explains, the process of healing will take work, but the effort will be totally worthwhile. Thank you, Jan Frazier, for bringing clarity and hope to my journey to become a fully realized adult, one who appreciates the child within but accepts the responsibilities of an adult to make life truly rewarding.

– Christy Loy, secondary teacher

D1496337

Through J. E. Frazier's intensely personal account of her ever-continuing journey to discover, understand, accept, and love herself, she hopes to aid others who may be traveling a similar road without much direction. Frazier shares the inspiration and help she has received from many professionals and then applies this knowledge to situations and conflicts of her own. The reader follows the path of her life as she struggles to heal her "wounded inner child" and to overcome the effects of being an adult child of an alcoholic. The book offers a good, insightful read plus encouragement to others who find themselves in similar struggles.

– Karen Smith, Guidance Counselor

Nice, easy read. Couldn't put it down once I started. Written by one of the very few teachers I liked in high school. Hard to believe she has inner demons too.

– Cindy J. Cornwellon

Jan Frazier has given not only herself the gift of healing her wounded Inner Child but she has also done the work of past and future generations. The best gift she could give people she loves is her own personal growth. Here is Jan's gift to her readers AND to all who have loved her, past, present, and future.

– Cleone Reed, MSE

Healing My Wounded Inner Child

A Journey to Wholeness

Jan E. Frazier

Robert D. Reed Publishers • Bandon, OR

Robert D. Reed Publishers
P.O. Box 1992
Bandon, OR 97411
Phone: 541-347-9882; Fax: -9883
E-mail: 4bobreed@msn.com
Website: www.rdrpublishers.com

ISBN: 978-1-934759-96-7
Library of Congress Number: 2015936169

Cover photo: Jan Frazier
Cover Designer: Cleone Reed
Interior Designer: Susan Leonard

Manufactured, typeset, and printed
in the United States of America

Foreword

After many years of counseling, I have finally accepted the fact that I'll always have to deal with my past childhood—my wounded Inner Child. Even when a "light" would go on after a counseling session and I would reach a plateau, I was still going to experience valleys in the future. My wounded Inner Child would never be totally healed, but most of the time, today, I am in a place in my life in which I feel safe and secure. Once in a while, I'll dip to the depths, but it doesn't happen often.

Dr. E. Kabatay gave me strength and guidance though some difficult times in my life, and I'll always be grateful to her for that. However, she always warned me that there would be ups and downs throughout life. When I was "flying high" after discovering and understanding hidden emotions and finding an additional healing mechanism for my Inner Child, I didn't believe the doctor. I thought that I was completely healed and that nothing could touch me. However, I always dropped from that plateau into a valley (it may have taken months or years, but it would happen), and I then remembered the good doctor's words. I would never be totally healed.

I still strive for approval, validation, and perfection. I often take myself too seriously, hide my anger, and become super-responsible. I judge myself too harshly and am loyal to people even when I shouldn't be. However, I'm better than I used to be... most of the time.

I struggled with writing this book, and yet it was a healing mechanism for me. I didn't know if I wanted to expose myself and share the secrets of my childhood about which only a few people knew. However, I decided that if I could help just one person who read the book, then it would be well worth the sacrifice. If you are one of those people struggling with a wounded Inner Child, there is hope for you. You may not know that you even have an Inner Child, but if you are enticed by the idea, I urge you to read this book (followed by every book that you can find that will help in the healing process). You are the only one who can really make a difference in your life. Doctors and counseling are readily available, but you have to do your homework by reading and seeking information, and then you are the one who brings home the success. It can be a long road, but there is light (even a bright light from time to time) along the way.

My greatest healing is that I have reached peace with my mother. From the start, I want to say that this book is not to belittle my mother in any way. I have to tell what I went through during my childhood in order for you, the readers, to understand how I had to reach out to my Inner Child and heal her. You, the reader, can do exactly the same.

I know in my heart that my mother didn't mean to hurt me. The majority of the time, she was totally unaware of hurting me. She was wrapped in her own grief (that of losing a son). In addition to that, I don't believe that she had a good childhood, and she was, undoubtedly, struggling with that herself (perhaps unknowingly). She had a wounded Inner Child who needed rescuing, but, of course, neither my mother nor I understood that during my growing-up years.

I so wish that she and I had the chance to reconcile our differences, and that I could have said, "Mom, I love you just the way that you are." However, from what I know of God's love, she understands that because she is in Heaven enjoying the pure goodness, mercy, and love of our Lord.

Last of all, I urge you to seek God's guidance, for He is the ultimate Healer. He is available 24/7 and loves you even when you think no one else does.

NOTE ABOUT NAMES: You may wonder why I became Janie in the book rather than Jan. I changed everyone's name in the book and pondered over using my real name Janice or not. Ultimately, I decided on Janie for a significant reason. My mother was originally going to name me Janie Elaine, but my aunt (who had been married ten years and was unable to conceive) talked her into Janice Elaine. I think that my mother liked the name Janice but didn't love it. I often question why she didn't stay with Janie Elaine (I would have been happier with Janie rather than Janice). However, my parents called me Jan and that was fine.

At any rate, the following year, my aunt became pregnant and was upset that my mom had taken "her" name! She ended up naming her daughter Janet Elaine. Thus, for a long time, I was Big Jan and my cousin was Baby Jan. When Baby Jan became ten, she developed an attitude about being Baby Jan, so she progressed to Jan and I became Janie. Thus, my relatives knew me as Janie, and often my mother would call me Janie.

I decided, therefore, to use the name that my mother really wanted to name me... Janie.

Healing My Wounded Inner Child

A Journey to Wholeness

CHAPTER 1

Remembrances of a Four-Year-Old

I sat in the corner of our small, modest living room, my knees pulled up under my plaid skirt. As my mother busied herself with the vacuuming, my eyes searched the room for my Dickie Doll. *He can sit on my lap with me so I won't be alone*, I thought. Silly, though, because I'd be afraid to leave my corner even if I saw my doll across the room. Not because I'd be scolded if I got up—it was fear of leaving the security of the corner; the small of my back was pushed rigidly against the wall. My eyes followed my mother's every movement as she vacuumed the room for a second time.

I was nearly four years old, and it had been a year and a half since my brother's death. He was nine, and I was two when he complained that he was too tired to ride the 12 blocks on his bike from home to school. It was 1949, and the doctors reported to my parents that it was the fastest growing, most acute case of leukemia that they had ever seen. Sent 150 miles away to a well-known children's hospital in Chicago, my mother sat at Harry's bedside for eight weeks. My aunt and uncle took over the duties of caring for the rambunctious two-year-old, who never sat still even in the high chair, feet constantly turning in a circular motion. My dad's long hours at the office during the weekdays and his weekend trips to Chicago to be with my dying brother kept me from spending much time with him as well.

However, my aunt, uncle, and 13-year-old cousin lived on a farm, and my days were soon filled with interesting events—sitting on the milk cows, playing with the kittens in the barn, exploring the open fields with my cousin, and playing with Bobby's trucks and tractors as we sat on the concrete slab in the backyard. It must have been a fun eight weeks as I was doted on by not only by aunt, uncle, and cousin, but also by all of my mother's family who tried to make life "normal" for me. They were losing their nephew—a beautiful nine-year-old boy who fit the picture of a perfect child—and I, unknowingly, was losing my beloved brother.

Harry had been my protector since my precarious, premature birth. With my mother hemorrhaging internally, I was taken C-section two months early. Even when I came home from the hospital before my mother, who had to recuperate for a month under doctor's care, my brother, aunt from Indiana, and Dad watched over me. Harry was the one to whom I clung from morning to night.

Now, as I sat in the corner at age four, I thought I had done something horrible, unspeakable, to make my mother ignore me—changing from a loving parent to one who wouldn't cuddle or caress. Engrossed in cleaning, she worked endlessly on the house until my dad came home. I waited to hear the car door slam in the garage and knew that the atmosphere of the day would soon change. My mom—who had been silent all day—would talk now to both my dad and me. If only I had understood that my mother's silent moods weren't directed towards me—that I wasn't the bad child whom she was punishing and ignoring—but rather it was an unhealthy way of dealing with the pain of losing a child. It was the only way she knew to cope—burying herself in her thoughts and tears. Her anguish far out-weighed mine, but I had no way of knowing or understanding.

The minister had lovingly consoled her with the thought that Harry had been too good for this earth, and she clung to that idea, obsessing on the sadness of losing an "angel." Mental anguish consumed her daily, and dealing with it was too much for her. Friends said she changed after Harry's death—she withdrew from them socially and was angry with life (maybe God, too) that her son was gone. Psychologists were not socially acceptable in those days, so as she withdrew more and more into herself, so did I. With two more years in the house with her, by the time I reached first grade, I wouldn't talk.

❧

CHAPTER 2

Insecure and Seeking Perfection

I had little contact with the outside world from the age of two until six. With only one car in the household in those days, there was no way of going shopping (malls didn't exist anyway), playing with friends (of which I had none because there were no children in the neighborhood), or having any type of social interaction with people. Until I was five, I don't remember much interaction even with my mother although I'm sure that wasn't the case. My mom fulfilled my physical needs and, undoubtedly, tried to fulfill my emotional needs; however, she was a broken person on the inside and life was difficult for her. My immature mind believed that I was a horrible child (I must be if even my mother didn't really love me), and I remember that my greatest fear was that she would leave me.

I had dreams of being left in the neighborhood grocery store to fend for myself and find my way home. I tried to talk to my aunt about my dreams, but she brushed them off saying, "Oh, Janie, your mother would never do such a thing." That was little consolation for an insecure, frightened child in a world that I found terrifying. I hated to take my naps for fear that my mother would be gone when I got up. One time I awoke and couldn't find her. She was outside in the yard, but I was in a tearful, frantic fit until I found her. Now that I was an only child without my brother's protection and companionship, I was spending those formative years in terror.

It was no wonder that at the age of six, I was socially insecure and unable to communicate with either adults or children. To say the least, the first-grade teacher was at a total loss as to what to do with me. What do you do with a child too shy to utter even a word? My mother finally was urged by the teacher to take me to a psychologist. After a few weeks of questioning, his diagnosis was that I was too afraid to make friends because they may leave me as my brother had. It was many years later that I realized my fear was connected to my mother. Thinking that I was a bad child, my own insecurity haunted my every thought, and I worried that my mom would leave me. Even at that age, I was trying my hardest to please her—to be perfect for her. I thought that perhaps if I could achieve perfection, I would have a mother who would truly love me. In reality, my mom did truly love me; but by then, my Inner Child had been wounded, and the image I had of myself was horribly distorted.

My classmates seemed to accept the fact that I wasn't going to talk in school, but the teacher was still searching for an answer to the perplexing problem that plagued her classroom (her Master's thesis was done on "the silent child"). Years later, she told me that she had tried everything but to no avail.

I found solace in one friend, Krista (who still remains my best friend today… 59 years later), and she and I played on the playground and walked home together after school. Krista was my sole link to the outside world. Krista was the "middle-man" who told the teacher my thoughts, which I didn't have the courage to share myself. What would have happened to me that first year of school without my friend, Krista?

On occasion, the teacher would say to me, "Janie, you look afraid. Are you afraid? Class, doesn't she look afraid?"

I'd want to hide under my desk. Not only did I not want her to call attention to me, but I also thought to myself… yes, I'm afraid; I'm petrified. To me, the world was a scary place, and all I knew was that I was terrified of life and what it had to offer. Not once at that time did I think that I was frightened of my mom. I loved her too much and longed for her unconditional love in return. I didn't know the source of my fear, but it was real and all-consuming.

Years later I read of the importance of those formative years (ages 0–6). Those years were of paramount importance in producing a well-adjusted child. In several of his books, John Bradshaw outlines the learning energies of a child during his/her formative years:

- Anger, sex and emotional energy
- Epigenetic development (each stage builds upon the previous one)
- Mirroring, echoing, affirming
- Touching, warmth, strokes, belonging, attachment
- Selfness, self-esteem, self-acceptance, self-actualization
- Autonomy, difference, space, separation
- Pleasure, pain, stimulation
- Dependability, predictability

I (like all children who live with a parent who is not able to function properly all of the time) suffered from lack of many of the *positive* energies that didn't exist in those formative years. In *The Homecoming*, Bradshaw states: "No parents in a dysfunctional family can give their child what he needs because they are too needy themselves. In fact, most children from dysfunctional families have been hurt the most when they were the most needy." The child can in no way imagine that there is anything wrong with his/her parent. For me at age four, my mother was the epitome of good and so her abandonment must have meant that something was horribly wrong with me. Abandonment is a form of abuse as Bradshaw explains in *Healing the Shame That Binds You*:

> Abuse is abandonment because when children are abused, no one is there for them... In each act of abuse the child is shamed. Young children, because of their egocentrism, make themselves responsible for the abuse. 'My caretakers couldn't be crazy or emotionally ill; it must be me,' the child says to himself. Children's minds are magical, egocentric, and non-logical, The children are completely dependent upon their parents for survival. 'If my parents are sick and crazy, how could I survive? It must be me.'

By now, of course, my mom had gotten through the first years after my brother's death. The stress, anguish, and loss were still present in a very real form, but more attention was being given to me. She was holding me now and talking to me as long as I did what she wanted me to do. Today, we call that "conditional love," but I only knew that I needed to make her happy because Harry was gone, and I was all that was left. I didn't want to "screw up"; however, I never reached that pinnacle of perfection that I wanted. I felt that I needed to succeed at everything that I did because maybe then my mother would be happy and would love me all the time.

I relished any compliment from her and all A's on my report card would usually get some recognition. After first grade, I talked in class, and teachers always praised me for my achievements as well as my good behavior. In spite of my shyness, I seemed to have many friends, and their parents seemed to enjoy having me at their homes. As I grew into fourth grade, I remember wanting to look nice at all times. "Janie, you always look perfect. You even have a lace hanky in your shirt pocket." Looking nice gained me recognition, but it still wasn't the total satisfaction for which I was seeking.

Yes, I was perfect but only on the outside. Perfection on the inside was inconceivable. To me, I was always the "bad" child whom my mother had ignored, and striving to perfect that inner being was constant. I would lie at night with my mind racing, trying to figure out the puzzle of how to validate my worthiness. It was as if an engine was running inside of me that wouldn't turn off. What could I do next to prove to my mother (and to myself) that I was good... not good, but the best?

My dad throughout all of this was always supportive in anything that I did, but still he never reprimanded my mother when I was given the "silent treatment" for not doing exactly what she wanted. I realize now that the "silent treatment" was Mom's way of dealing with what she felt was loss of control, but to me, I was just a bad child. I decided that perhaps even my dad thought that I was bad because he seemed to support my mom's behavior.

Regardless of all of that, my dad was the person whom I adored. He was kind, caring, funny, gregarious, and loving—the person whom I wanted to emulate. Always in my mind's eye, my dad was the perfect role model, and even to this day, I wish that I could be like him.

Socially, by the time I was eight or ten, my mother had started to interact with her old friends, and apparently they quit worrying about her. Everything had worked out after all. Anna (although never regaining her old self) was active in church again, and Janie had developed into a nice little girl even though she was far too shy. Of course, everyone realized that it was horribly difficult to lose a child, but families continued and life went on.

For me, though, life had stood still since the age of four when I sat on the floor of the living room, trying to understand why I had been so bad. I was still the little girl that was ignored and unwanted, but now I was striving for perfection—an impossible feat at any age. I was now the child who had to be perfect for not only my mother but also for me.

❦

CHAPTER 3

Anorexia Nervosa: A Young Girl's Nightmare

Teenage years were difficult (as they are for all children and parents as well), but I never felt the need to rebel (outwardly, at least). I always believed that I mustn't disobey or disappoint my parents because they had lost a son, and I was all that was left. I shouldn't cause them more anguish, especially my mother whom I knew already was emotionally fragile. I needed to make them proud and my achievements generally showed that. Only my mother's lack of loving, supportive words were missing.

I realize as I look back at my teenage years, I was no "angel." I was mouthy and outspoken at times. I even believe that my mom must have praised me at times. However, because I was still stuck with the four-year-old wounded Inner Child, I couldn't see the good times which, undoubtedly, did exist.

For me, it was a complex love/hate relationship (not so unusual, I guess, for a teenager). I hated her for trying to control me, for giving me the "silent treatment," and for "abandoning" me as a child. But still I loved her and continually sought her approval. Already my co-dependency was well established (see Chapter 9 concerning co-dependency).

Inwardly, however, I was already experiencing intestinal trouble. In fifth grade, I was diagnosed with a "nervous colon" and had to lie down often after meals. Eating had been something that I really didn't enjoy even at an early age, and now it was even more of a problem. "Come on; let's take a walk around the block, and I'll make you a milk shake to drink," my mother would suggest, a sure sign that she really did love and care for me. Okay, that worked, but I was still thin and pale, and, of course, my mother worried that I would be next to die of leukemia.

Truly, I regret that there was no counseling available because I *now* believe that my mom loved me but felt insecure and scared herself. She was still wrought with anxiety over my brother's death, and a counselor would have helped all of us. What my mother battled on the inside, I'll never know. She kept everything to herself, never discussing her feelings with me or even with my dad. Being raised in a totally German family, my mom was taught to fight her own battles and not seek consolation from others.

* * *

I guess that it was during college years that I knew that probably nothing that I'd do would really make my mother happy... grades, achievements, or awards. I was too old to have my every move controlled by her. I wanted some freedom and needed some wheels.

My first car that I bought with money that I had put aside from after-school and summer jobs was a used Chevy convertible. I experienced the "silent treatment" for many weeks after that because I was far too young to have a car (I was 19, and I needed a way to and from the university in a nearby city). My dad had seen my plight, and to my delight, he had helped me find the car. At last I had a way to escape from the control that I felt was unending and the life that I felt I had endured too long.

It must have been during this time that I uncon-sciously realized that I had complete control over what I ate. No longer could my mother force me to eat and ridicule me for not eating what she wanted me to eat. Actually, she couldn't make me do anything that I didn't want to do… I was an "adult."

Anorexia Nervosa was not yet diagnosed in 1968, but it didn't mean that it didn't exist. It was and is a terrible disease… not only for the parents but also for the child. I ate little and exercised continually in order to get my already slim-framed, 5-foot 7-inch body to 98 pounds. Again, the motor raced inside of me, push-ing me to limits that I never knew existed. Up early in the morning and staying awake late into the night, I read and re-read my college texts and studied my notes incessantly in order to get straight A's. I had no social life (now I wondered why did I need that car?… surely, it was only for transportation to school) because I was obsessed with my schoolwork. Studying to be a secondary teacher, I had to be the best—I had to be perfect.

Of course, now anorexia nervosa is recognized, and I realize that I was a prime candidate:

- You are a white teenage girl.
- You are a perfectionist (yes, definitely).
- You are suffering from anxiety (yes, I needed perfect grades... that was anxiety!).
- You have symptoms of depression (yes, I was unhappy with myself... perfection couldn't be attained, plus as with all girls suffering from anorexia, I saw myself as fat).
- Tremendous psychological torment (grades, validations, responsibilities, self-esteem, codependency, self-acceptance, unworthiness, and the list goes on... notice that all of these concepts were placed on me mostly by me personally).
- You are obsessed exercising and *not* eating.
- You have a controlling mother (indeed, yes!).

Now there is help for the girl with anorexia nervosa. There are centers where she can go to be diagnosed and learn to eat properly. However, in the 1960s, there was nothing but criticism for the girl who wouldn't eat... criticism from the mothers as well as the doctors (who had no clue as to what to do with an underweight, "rebellious" teenage girl).

Of course, my mother was in a constant state of worry about my health, and I remember (in my immature way of thinking) that I was glad that she was fretting. If I couldn't get positive attention, at least I knew how to get negative attention. I was thrown headlong into the teenage disease that claimed hundreds of girls' lives.

Probably I would have starved myself to death had I not been diagnosed as hypoglycemic and hospitalized. With my blood sugar falling to 35 (death was 30), I was teetering on a brink, and I knew that I had to eat now in order to live. And, in reality, I did want to live, but I wanted control of my own life and desired to be out from under my mother. By now, my life was centered around becoming an educator, and by the time I started teaching in 1971, I had reached a grand weight of 107 pounds. Even though I was still very thin, I was on the road to recovery from the terrible disease of Anorexia Nervosa.

℘

CHAPTER 4

Adult Child of an Alcoholic

Now came the only period of time that I can remember really rebelling (at that time, I didn't see not eating as being rebellious). With the money I had saved after the first year of teaching, I started to travel to Europe and met a young man abroad. Looking back now, I realize that I was determined to get away from my mother and *that* I did… 3,000 miles away. I married a European and moved across the Atlantic. It was an excellent time for me to grow up—a new culture, a new husband, a new lifestyle, and a new language. Wow, life was suddenly very different. I began to realize what I had had at home and also became aware of what it was like to be an adult, making my own decisions. I didn't always like it. Still inside, I was the little girl who was lost and unwanted, searching for why I was bad.

This separation was good for my mother, too. She had a chance to think of how our relationship could improve, and her letters and phone calls were warm and loving. I felt as if things could really be different if we were together again. Maybe we both had grown although my own self-concept hadn't changed too much. For the first time, though, I had hope that I could please my mom and that we could be "friends."

Her visit to Europe, however, was "just like old times." She, my dad, and aunt stayed with my husband and me for three weeks. After the first week, Mom had "settled in" and the criticism started: Europe was awful (so behind America in its old-world ways), my curtains were wrong, the refrigerator wasn't adequate, my husband was stupid, my job would get me nowhere, the food wasn't good and too expensive, toilet paper wasn't soft enough, the cars were too small... the list was endless. It was the only time that I saw my dad get angry at my mother... really angry. He pushed her against the wall and yelled, "Shut up!"

After a stage of pouting (and complete shock that my dad had yelled at her), my mother wanted to go home. We took her to the airport to try to change her ticket, and there she made an embarrassing scene that even humiliated the airline clerk. She proceeded to tell him how awful his country was, finally ending with a recount of the faults of her daughter who lived in this terrible, uncivilized place. It was an understatement to say that we were all mortified. After all was said and done, she couldn't change her ticket without paying an additional 200 dollars so she stayed. For the most part, it was an unbearable two more weeks.

Two years later, my moving back to the States was good, but relocating eventually in my hometown was not. Unfortunately (and stupidly), I fell back into the old patterns of letting my mother control many of my decisions (co-dependency won out again), and eventually my marriage failed (partially because of these circumstances; after all, who would want three in a marriage? But more on this later).

Some years later, I read a book entitled *Toxic Parents* by Dr. Susan Forward which explained to me that, unfortunately, I was still very "enmeshed" with my parents, a very self-defeating role. If I could answer "yes" to four of the following, I was having problems being an independent person. I answered "yes" to all of them:

- It is up to me to make my parents happy.
- It is up to me to make my parents proud.
- I shouldn't do or say anything that would hurt my parents' feelings.
- There's no point in talking to my parents because it wouldn't do any good.
- If my parents would only change, I would feel better about myself.
- My parents' feelings are more important than mine.

Not only was I having trouble being a "separate" person, but also my parents (or rather, my mother) played the role of "toxic parent." In other words, if my mother felt bad, then somehow I was burdened with the blame. She wouldn't have to say that, but I felt it.

Words that my mom used to say during my childhood would pour into my thoughts at night: "You'll be the death of me; you're a disgrace to me; someday you'll get yours; I hope that I live long enough to see this happen to you; shame on you—how could you do this to me? You certainly know how to cut my heart out, don't you?" The list went on and on, and they were all phrases that would automatically put the blame on me for *her* feelings. Again, if only counseling had been available when I was a child, life could have been different for everyone.

At any rate, after the divorce, I was left with two children to raise. Fortunately for me, I fell in love with a man who also surprisingly loved me and wanted to adopt my children, and I remarried. Later in life, I found that he had some of the same controlling qualities of my mother, but he was an excellent father to my children, a good provider, and I loved him.

However, by then at the age of 35, internally, I was in turmoil. Because of gastrointestinal problems, allergies, backaches, and insomnia, my medical doctor suggested that I see a psychologist to help me through my childhood problems, which seemed to continually resurface. Readily, I agreed. I was willing to try anything. However, I was unprepared to hear what the doctor said after talking to me for just ten minutes.

"Who in your family has a drinking problem?"

A drinking problem? In my immediate family there was no one, but I knew that I had a cousin who was an alcoholic and my ex-husband had become one. I was sent home with a list of books to purchase about "adult children of alcoholics" and told to return in two weeks. My last question as I left the office was, "How can I be an adult child of an alcoholic if my parents don't drink?"

"Someone on your mother's side of the family did, and it has affected your mother. Find out who it was."

I delved into those books as if my life depended upon them (and I guess that it did). I knew from the first chapters that the authors of the books were definitely talking directly to me. In two days, I had read every word from the prescribed books as I had stayed up nights voraciously reading. I poured over the books and the questions they raised:

- Do you guess at what "normal" is?
- Do you have difficulty having fun?
- Do you judge yourself mercilessly?
- Are you a perfectionist?
- Do you take yourself too seriously?
- Do you constantly seek approval and validation?
- Are you super-responsible?
- Are you extremely loyal, even when loyalty isn't deserved?
- Are you impulsive?
- Do you hide your anger?

The answer to the questions was 100 percent "Yes." Finally someone could possibly explain my complex childhood (which I had never discussed with anyone except with my husband), my inner drive, my longing for validation, and my striving to be perfect. I had no idea that not only was there someone else on earth with the same problems but also books had been written about them!

But who was an alcoholic in the family? I had one aunt (the one who cared for me when I came home prematurely from the hospital and who also had visited me in Europe) who I felt might give me some straight answers. I knew that my mother would deny everything, and it was not a topic about which I wanted to discuss with her because she and I only talked of superficial subjects... never personal topics.

At first my aunt also denied any alcoholism, but off-handedly she added at the end of our conversation, "Well, my grandpa was an alcoholic, but he wasn't related by blood." I wanted to scream, "What do you mean? He was your grandpa! Of course, he was blood relation." Denial seemed to be something at which my mother's family was good, and my aunt's comment followed suit. That was the only time I talked to my aunt about the subject, but I had gotten my answer.

As I read more books, I realized that a person doesn't have to grow up with an alcoholic but only live with someone who has grown up with one in order to become an adult child of an alcoholic. Traits are passed down from generation to generation. My great-grandfather had been an alcoholic. He had possibly been both physically and emotionally abusive, definitely uncontrollable in his actions, and totally unpredictable in his mood swings. All alcoholics are. Alcohol controls their very being, and families, of course, always suffer severely. Denial usually starts with denying that a drinking problem even exists.

My grandmother and her siblings must have all lived on the edge. When would their father explode over nothing? He was, undoubtedly, a time bomb. Would he decide to hit one of the children? What insane act would he do next? Worst of all, no one could confront him. Each person in the household lived in constant fear of not knowing what to expect next.

My grandmother was one of his children and grew up under these conditions, passing those same behaviors on to her children. She had learned the exact personality characteristics and learned them well. Even as a child, I knew my grandmother had had unpredictable behavior. My mother always kept the back door to our house unlocked because Grandma would explode if she walked the half block to our home to find it locked. My mother feared and disliked her. Because of my grandmother's adult-child behavior, my mother was still an adult child herself, continuing the actions that she had been taught, and she was passing them along to me.

Now, for the first time, I had a brief insight into my mother's actions. She had been a frightened adult child herself, trying to cope with the death of my brother, attempting to raise me during her uncontrollable mourning, and laying the tracks that had been laid for her during infancy. But I also realized now that my brother's death only added to my mother's problems and that she had been an adult child *before* he died. All of what happened to me would have occurred anyway (even if he had lived) but maybe not to the extent that it did. Now, I had to admit that I, too, was an adult child.

I reflected on a time—and this incident only happened *one* time, never to be mentioned again—that my mother broke down and cried, saying, "You have no idea what I did to your brother in the years before he died." It was the only clue that I was ever to receive that she knew of her cruel behavior. She must have made him feel like a "bad" child, too, and now the guilt was unbearable for her.

Suddenly, it was all clear. I wasn't really "bad" and neither was my brother. Because my mom was an adult child of an alcoholic, she carried the burden that she herself was unworthy and "bad." She was unable to show true love to others because she didn't love herself. Unconditional love was an impossible feat for my mom to achieve.

Even Harry—who now in my mother's mind was "perfect"—must have suffered through the bad-child years as well. Of course, I thought, why would he have escaped her wrath? Just because he's perfect in her mind now, doesn't mean that he wasn't a normal child just like me. Somehow, none of this had ever crossed my mind. Had Harry lived, he, too, would have been an adult child like me.

* * *

I realized, too, as I continued to understand the problem that my physical state was being overruled by my emotional state. The digestive problems had started in childhood and continued into adulthood. By allowing anger at my mother to become internalized, I had suffered eating disorders, illnesses, and chronic gastrointestinal problems. Even then I couldn't tell my mother when I was angry for fear of the silent treatment, and I didn't even live with her any longer. What sense did that make? Inside, I was still the child who feared her mother's dislike... I was still the bad little girl, age four.

But questions were being answered for me. I now understood why I had to be "superwoman"—I needed to receive validation and positive comments from people. It made me feel worthy, accomplished, and most of all loved. I also now understood why I couldn't show anger towards anyone for any reason—I might lose that person's friendship, and I needed that most of all. *I'll take the blame... I probably deserve it anyway,* I always thought. Finally, I understood why it was difficult to have fun with my own children—there just was little time for fun and games. After all, I was too busy trying to be perfect and that was a serious job.

I remembered that my mother always had said she had to get her work done first before she could play with me. I thought it was her German upbringing (work first; play later), but now I knew differently. I found that with my mom, the work was never done (always something to be cleaned... if not once, then twice), and there was never time for fun. She didn't *know* how to have fun. No wonder that I never really learned that trait, and, thus, I couldn't achieve having fun with my children.

Incredibly, though, many people didn't see me the way I really was. I'm fairly sure that I was a good teacher, and the students often asked for me the next semester. They even told me that I was fun to have as a teacher in class (I'm not sure how that happened). However, I was a careful grader and expected the students to work (not be perfect, however... that was saved for me). I had many friends, was gregarious (at last), and was exceedingly responsible (of course, I had to be perfect!).

However, as I continued to read book after book and started going to counseling on a regular basis, I knew that the tracks of the adult child of the alcoholic had definitely been laid, and they were in place and solid. I had a big job ahead of me.

✀

CHAPTER 5

A Marriage Gone Wrong

I have to take time here to look at my failed marriage. It failed before I ever went to counseling so I was floundering in the dark most of the time. My self-esteem was low; I didn't like myself; I was co-dependent. None of these aspects make for a successful marriage. I look for the exact reasons, though, as to why it failed. Definitely, I will take more than half of the blame. I allowed my mother to become a threesome in a marriage built for two. That was totally my fault, and I knew it (not at the time, but I do now). But there were other circumstances as well.

After three to four years in the States, my European husband had become an alcoholic and a womanizer. I now had some of the same difficulties with my husband as I had had with my mother. His behavior mirrored the adult-child-of-an-alcoholic behavior of my mother. Unfortunately, that seemed okay at the start of our marriage. After all, that was the lifestyle to which I was familiar. However, I eventually saw his behavior as not only something with which I couldn't live but also a behavior with which I didn't want my own children growing up. He was unpredictable (of course, he had been drinking); he made irrational decisions, he was emotionally abusive, and he put the blame on me for everything that went wrong. Wow... I had married my mother!

Statistics show that most adult children will marry someone who continues the "comfortable" yet abusive lifestyle to which they are accustomed. They don't like it, yet it's the only way they have ever lived. It's a sad, unfortunate truth that happens to most adult children.

Nevertheless, true to form, at the beginning of our marriage, I was willing to sacrifice my happiness to stay in the marriage. After all, I only knew from past experiences that my sole purpose was to make the caretaker happy at all costs. I needed to live with circumstances the way they were because I was the "bad" person, and things would be better if only I could make them right.

Of course, I had not only my alcoholic husband with whom to deal, but I also had my mother at the other end, telling me that I was stupid, worthless, and unacceptable because I continued to live with such a man. "You know that I hated him from the start, and you had to make the stupid mistake of marrying him. I'm not going to quit until you get a divorce so you're going to have to make it right. Here's what you need to do..." And with that, her tirade would begin.

Truthfully, with turmoil on all sides, I now wonder what *I* must have been like during those times. I couldn't have been the best mother. I know that I put far too much responsibility on my older daughter. I hardly left my children's sides, and so my older daughter was the all-too-convenient person to share many of my problems. That was one of my biggest mistakes of my life… one over which I had control, and I "blew it." I often talked to her as if she were an adult, pouring over my problems and aimlessly wondering aloud what I should do. I didn't expect answers from her… I needed someone with whom to share the many difficulties that I was facing.

This mistake of over-burdening my child with my adult problems still haunts me today, and, of course, any damage that was done to her during her "listening" sessions was irreversible. She and I discuss it from time to time, and with a forgiving heart, she says that she understands the perplexities of my life at that time.

I would have continued in this destructive marriage (I thought that I deserved the worst, you know), but an incident with my older daughter made me see the light. It was the evening before her sixth birthday, and her father came home drunk. I didn't want to expose my children to his behavior as he ranted around the house in a drunken state. I took them by their hands, and we went outside. Upon trying to re-enter the house, I found that he had locked us out and was sitting on the telephone (in full view), talking with his girlfriend, laughing hysterically that we were on the outside, and he was on the inside.

We went across the street to my neighbor (who was fully aware of my household situation) and called the police. It was 8 o'clock and my daughter had to get up for school the next morning… I wanted to get her to bed. When the police arrived, they tried to talk to him, but he was out of control. With the door still locked, he told the police that he would never lock his children out of their home. The police demanded that the door be opened.

He did, but the police advised me not to go into the house when he was in his state of drunkenness. Determinedly, I said, "He will not keep me or my children from entering my home. I'm not afraid of him." With that, I took the children to their rooms, and I think that he left for his girlfriend's house. The rest of the night was a blur, but I *still* didn't know that I should withdraw from the marriage. Not until the next morning…

It was my daughter's birthday, and as she was leaving for the bus, I put her jacket on her and said, "Honey, you have a fabulous birthday today."

Her answer still reverberates in my mind. "Mommy, I could never have a good birthday today."

That's all that needed to be said. That afternoon, I visited a lawyer. When my husband reappeared a few days later (to get clothes, I guess, to take with him to his girlfriend's apartment), I told him our marriage was over.

"What's so different from the other times?" he asked in surprise. "I don't want a divorce. I want a girlfriend as well as a wife."

I didn't seem to mind that he was ruining my life, but he would *never* destroy my children's lives. I wouldn't allow that. My children saved me from continuing in a marriage that would have been my physical as well as emotional collapse. Even my minister applauded me for getting out of the marriage not only for the children's sakes but also for mine. "He committed adultery, and God does not want you to stay in a faithless marriage." For once, I could see the light.

My older daughter had taught me a lesson that I wouldn't forget—take care of us children as well as yourself. I had always taken care of my children but not myself. It was the first of many lessons that my children taught me.

If a mother will listen carefully, she will find that her children teach her the most valuable of all lessons in life. I read once that a parent can learn as much from her child as the child can from the parent. Children are the *wisest* of all teachers. They are innocent, see things so much more clearly than adults, say things exactly as they should be said (no frills or cover-ups), never intend to be hurtful—only honest—and want only love and protection in return. When I listened carefully, I found that their innocent, child-like wisdom was astounding.

CHAPTER 6

%

Struggles with the Inner Child

As the years progressed, there were many times that I thought that I was "healed," that I was being a really good mom and wife, and that I had all of my "ducks in a row." I'd have incredibly happy intervals in my life, and I'd think, "Well, I'm over the hump." And then something would happen—one of my children got out of control, I failed at a task, or someone got mad at me—and I'd know that I wasn't "healed" but just in a transition stage and needed more work.

It wasn't until my children were grown and started to "fly the nest" that a certain amount of depression set in. I don't remember ever being depressed while they were small. It wasn't just depression, though, because there was also a continual "drive" that kept me up for hours working on a project, followed later by some depression. I believe the "drive" had always been there even as a child—it kept the wheels moving as I strived to be "the best." However, now I had so much time extra time on my hands since my children had grown up and had left home, and—as mothers know—we miss the constant interaction with our children.

I was back at the doctor's doorstep, looking again for answers. Was your mother depressed? Yes, often. Did she too drive herself unmercifully? Yes, of course—that's a characteristic of an adult child, isn't it? Yes, the highs and lows, the unexpected behavior, the drive—they are characteristic of adult children, but she could have possibly been bipolar. Was she bipolar? I don't know; later, she was diagnosed as clinically depressed. Am I bipolar? I don't know. I hope not.

Finally diagnosed as "depressed at times with hyperactivity," I knew that I had mood swings from time to time, especially after my children were grown and had left home, and I didn't like it. Put on an anti-depressant, it seemed to help. Going in spurts, I'd read book after book on self-help, always seeking answers and trying to better myself (I still desired perfection… a great clue that I wasn't cured). Sometime along the way, I had begun to read about the wounded Inner Child, and again from the first page, I knew that I had come upon something that was meant for me.

I started buying only books that dealt with uncovering the lost child who was hiding within me. I learned that I could communicate with this little child inside. In one book that I read—*The Family* by John Bradshaw—I found some answers:

There is strong agreement that the children we once were live in us as a complete energy state of feelings, thoughts, and desires. If our developmental dependency needs were not met, the energy that would have accrued in the resolution of each developmental stage is blocked.

I learned the things to say to my wounded Inner Child, and I talked to her (on occasion), trying to heal her:

- You can count on me being here for you.
- I'm glad that you're a girl.
- I want to hold you.
- I love you just as you are.
- Everything about you is okay with me.
- I want to take care of you.
- Hold my hand, and we'll work everything out together.

I pictured myself sitting with my Dickie Doll with my plaid skirt on at the age of four, and I'd be happy (for a while). If I didn't keep up with the ritual, though, I'd fall back into depression or hyperactivity, but no one would know the better for it (of course, except for me) because I had a good "cover." Sometimes, I felt the loneliness, emptiness, unrest, insecurity, unworthiness, and helplessness throughout my being. If I could continue to be a good actress, however, no one would ever know. After all, teachers have to be good actresses. We're in front of 130 students every day, and we need to smile, be happy, full of enthusiasm, and willing to teach. One of my colleagues in the secondary school used to say, "When the bell rings, the curtain goes up." Basically, that was true...we had to "play the part" and act well. However, *I* did not want to "play a part" all of the time and wanting to correct that flaw became paramount in my life.

The more I learned about the wounded Inner Child, the more I wanted to know. The child inside wanted to heal. She was childish and had lacked the proper nourishment as an infant. Often she would polarize, thinking to extremes. Everything was either/or, no in-between. For the child inside of me, the world was a frightful place in which to live.

There was a voracious neediness of my Inner Child. Because of scarcity of loving strokes and enjoyment early in infancy, I craved them now and would go overboard. I wanted my children always near me, needed to be with people continually, strived for positive attention, and loved to go on shopping sprees. It was all due to the need of instant gratification.

And then there was the problem of taking on too much responsibility. I only knew how to be the "super-woman" because as a child, I needed to prove myself not only to my mother but also to me. Every job gave me responsibility as well as validation from people who marveled at the number of tasks I performed with such precision.

Throughout all of my struggles with my Inner Child, somehow I continually placed my trust in God and felt that someday I'd be able to cope with my past as well as with my Inner Child. God had brought me through so much, and even though I still didn't see myself as "good," I knew that He would stay with me throughout the turmoil—that He actually loved me unconditionally. I could only pray that one day it would all become clear and the light at the end of the tunnel would suddenly flood my world.

CHAPTER 7

My "Normal" Life

And so as you read this, you possibly think...this poor woman had no life, was friendless; she was confused, sad, overworked, and depressed. Nothing could be further from the truth (at least on the outside). In reality, when I was depressed or even hyper, no one knew (except maybe my immediate family). After all, I had lived through abusive times in my infancy and struggled throughout my childhood. I had survived all of them when I was little, and I had been *alone* in the chaos. Of course, by now as an adult, I was already a *survivor* and could cover most everything with a laugh and smile.

I looked to be a happy person (and many times, I truly was). In fact, as long as "all my ducks were in a row," validation occurred for my accomplishments, tasks were completed as perfect as possible, and there were multiple projects "in the fire" to keep me from thinking, then I would have said that I was *completely* happy. I didn't really understand that underneath everything, the Inner Child was crying because she had too much responsibility placed upon her and that childhood issues were still brewing.

In reality, when all was said and done, the faculty at school liked me, I had miraculously become a people-person who loved to be around all kinds of people (friends as well as strangers), and my students seemed to enjoy me. Seldom did I have a problem with a student who might cause other teachers to want to commit suicide. Truly, I don't know how that happened.

In addition, I lived a fulfilling life by taking trips to Europe each year. I had lived there in my 20s and loved the old-world life. I seemed to always fit into that lifestyle and so every year I had 30 to 40 students and adults who wanted to go with me on a trip abroad. Year after year I thrived on sharing my knowledge of Europe, helping each student learn through travel, and teaching the young people to grow through knowledge of the world. I absolutely *lived* to take them abroad each summer.

I had a caring husband who loved me, and my children were beautiful and succeeded in school (well, most of the time). My parents were still married and *seemed* to have a fantastic life together (only outwardly, of course)... nice house, money, and security. Underneath, however, the turmoil continued.

My mother, by the time she was in her 70s, had started to withdraw from society. My dad, the talkative, gregarious person, spent much of his time drinking coffee and playing cards with his buddies, and my mother continued to clean her already-spotless house (unless the grandchildren visited... then she stopped everything for them. *Amazing,* I thought). The doctor put her on an anti-depressant, and she was a bit better. Her once-uncertain disposition became tolerable, and she seemed more mellow, calmer, less depressed, and far less explosive.

When my dad died suddenly, my husband and I reached out to my mother and took her to stay with us at night. During the daytime, she was fine alone, but she was terrified at night. Of course, she was still an adult child (with an incredibly wounded Inner Child), and so why wouldn't she be frightened? All inner children are terrified of the dangerous world that surrounds them, and her Inner Child had had no opportunity to heal at all. Of course, she wasn't even aware of an Inner Child. At least through counseling, mine had a glimpse of the "normal" and was striving in the right direction most of the time.

Although my mom had to eventually enter a nursing home, my husband and I visited once to twice a day, and I'm so glad we made that effort. She was my mother, after all, and had done the best she could considering her own, undoubtedly, traumatic past. The love/hate relationship had healed, and I loved her despite our differences.

Often at the nursing home, my mother would introduce me as her mom. "Have you met my mom?" she'd say to the nurses. The nurses and I would exchange glances and smiles, and I always wondered how she could be so confused. One day during the normal introduction, she stopped halfway through. "Oh, I guess she's my daughter. She takes care of me each day so I thought she was my mom." At last *that* mystery was solved. From then on, I always smiled when she introduced me as "Mom" and quickly added, "Yes, I'm Anna's mom."

Unfortunately, I never had the opportunity to work out problems of my past with my mother. I never asked her to go to counseling with me because I knew that she wouldn't. My dad had suggested that the three of us go for counseling when I was in junior high, and she told us to go alone… she didn't need help. In past years, I often have wished that my dad and I had gone alone. We could have learned so much and been better able to cope with our home life. Perhaps, we could have helped her. But we didn't pursue that course, and the topic of counseling was never again broached.

I wish now that I had said something to my mom that would have been non-threatening, non-accusing, such as "What was your childhood like, Mom? What was Grandma like when you were growing up? Did you know her father (your maternal grandpa—the alcoholic) well?" I should have asked my mom about *her* life—her pain, suffering, and abandonment by her own mother (which must have occurred). That's a change I wish I could make, but it's too late, and I'll never know the answers. I can only imagine what they would have been. Continually, my heart goes out to my mom because now I know she suffered more than I did.

I have read that parental influence is stronger from the grave than it is first hand, and I have to agree with that. My Inner Child at times cried out even louder after my mother was gone. I continued to counsel from time to time when life seemed to get the better of me, and I guess I thought that the Inner Child would heal and *stay* healed. I'd never have to work with her again. Nothing was further from the truth.

When I did early retirement after 25 years in secondary education, I returned to the university to finally finish my masters and then was asked to teach at my alma mater. I was thrilled to be teaching where I had attained both my bachelors and masters, and teaching college gave me the validation I needed. I had started to write novels at that time, became a public speaker to promote the educational value of travel and to speak on the Holocaust (a long-time interest of mine), did workshops at schools for my books, still went to Europe once or twice a year, taught full-time at the university, taught J-Term abroad in London for the university, and babysat on a part-time basis for my grandchildren. People would say, "How do you do everything that you do?" Actually, I loved it all, but I also found that I was sleeping less and less during my hyper times, and then once in a while I'd have the bottom fall out, and I'd become depressed.

"Forget your past," the doctor would tell me. "It's over and your mother is gone. You don't have to prove anything to her anymore. You've proven everything to yourself... what do you want?"

"Slow down," my husband would harp. "Why can't you relax and just sit? Watch a TV show."

The truth was that my Inner Child was *still* crying out, and, honestly, I didn't hear her so I filled my hours with work...workaholic, I think is the proper term. I had not yet learned the solution to really listening and learning from my Inner Child, so I continued to be the "superwoman" so that my life seemed fulfilled.

CHAPTER 8

A Breakthrough

And then I had a falling out with two friends during one of my hyper times. I was in Europe and stressed out to the maximum with driving on the European highways all day. I was alone with an over-stressed Inner Child when my two "friends" decided that three was a crowd, and I was the third wheel... funny because the "third wheel" was the sole driver and interpreter (not always a good one, I might add) of the three foreign languages that we needed on the trip. With better understanding of the Inner Child, I would have handled the situation differently, but I fell apart because someone was mad at me. I was "bad" because my two friends wouldn't talk to me. I digressed into my childhood and cried as if I was getting the "silent treatment" from my mother. I apologized to my friends for whatever I had done wrong (I had no idea why I was apologizing, but it seemed the right thing to do... after all, I would have apologized to my mother), and I cried some more.

In reality, we were "three children"—I was crying because I thought I was "bad," and they were in an even more child-like state, ignoring me and making me an outcast just as children do in a heartless moment of immaturity. In today's terms, they were full-fledged bullies. For six days I was a victim to their cruelty when, finally, on the last night, I allowed my Adult Being to surface, and I moved from their room into a room of my own so I was no longer the "third wheel." I had a bed of my own (instead of the mattress on the floor); I quit crying, and I felt good for standing up to two bullies.

When I returned home, I dragged out my books of self-help and started to re-read each of them. I poured over the ones on the Inner Child. Why was I still suffering from this silly Inner-Child thing? To me, though, it wasn't silly, and when I closed my eyes, I could visualize my Inner Child—she was inside and was still that little girl wearing the plaid skirt and sitting on the living room floor as she had when she was four years old. I started talking to that precious Inner Child again.

I re-read everything that I had learned before—that I should love, hold, and caress my Inner Child several times a day. I must listen to her needs and hear her when she was upset, telling her she was beautiful just the way she was and that she didn't need to change. I needed to love her for herself. I knew all of this from my previous readings; however, suddenly in the midst of re-reading, something became clear. That light at the end of the tunnel became blinding.

My wounded Inner Child (in her jutted infant state) was controlling and running my life. The little girl within was making all of my major decisions. She was terrified at being in charge; she made wrong choices many times, and she cried continually at being left to "run the show." The little child within was pushed into being overly-responsible, to perfecting every detail of my life, into smiling when she was hurting, and into making choices totally beyond her means. No wonder she was crying, being hyper, not able to sleep, depressed, and feeling inadequate...she was a child in an adult world, taking control of the decisions that my Adult Being should have been making. How could I have missed all of this when I first learned of my wounded Inner Child?

If my Adult Being had been in charge in Europe, I would have told my two "friends" to grow up. If I was the third wheel, apparently I wasn't needed, and they could find their own transportation and interpreter. But I didn't, and, in addition, I never lowered myself to their level by being cruel. Unfortunately, six days of my trip (and many other situations in my life) had been tainted because I had allowed the adult decision-making process to be placed on my Inner Child, and from that moment on, I knew that I'd try *not* to let my Inner Child be in charge of adult business.

Suddenly one of the meditations suggested by John Bradshaw in the book *Healing the Shame that Binds You* made sense:

- Embrace your lost Inner Child.

- Notice how she is dressed, what she looks like, every detail.
- Tell her that you are from her future.
- Tell her that you know better than anyone what she has been through.
- You know her suffering, abandonment, shame.
- You are the only one that she will never lose.
- Ask her if she is willing to go home with you.
- See your mom and dad come out and wave good-bye to them.
- See your Higher Power come into your life and heart and take charge.

I needed to coddle my Inner Child, protect and take care of her, allow her the pleasures of life, and not place the responsibilities of my everyday problems and trials on her shoulders. I alone knew her suffering, and I alone could comfort her. I needed to wave good-bye to my parents as *my* Adult Being was now in charge. I would never leave my Inner Child. Through thick and thin, we were bonded.

I continued to read pieces written by John Bradshaw that helped to further explain the Inner Child:

It is important to note that the need to find the Inner Child is part of every human being's journey toward wholeness. No one had a perfect childhood. Everyone bears the unresolved unconscious issues of his family history. The Inner Child's journey is the hero's journey. To find our Inner Child is the first leap over the abyss of grief that threatens us all. But finding the Inner Child is just the beginning. Because of his isolation, neglect and neediness, this child is egocentric, weak and frightened. He must be disciplined in order to release his tremendous spiritual power.

It was a breakthrough for me. I realized for the first time that my Adult Being had failed my Inner Child. I had given her adult responsibility and expected her to know what to do with it. Every book reiterated the same information as the one before, and for the first time I really started to understand the Inner Child concept. I stopped and thanked God for the falling out with the friends because that circumstance helped me to reach out once more for help and find answers.

Beverly Engel's book entitled *The Emotionally Abused Woman* said again what Bradshaw's books said, but nevertheless it helped to re-establish more solid thoughts on the Inner Child:

When emotional, physical, or sexual abuse occurs, children often regress in their development and revert back to a very primary developmental stage in order to survive. They may then be unable to progress in their development as they should. However, if you give yourself the security, comfort, and nurturing you missed as a child, you do not have to allow any impairments in your early development to interfere with your life today or with your ability to become an independent self. Be loving to yourself. Give yourself strokes, encouragement, and acknowledgment. Give yourself a lot of positive self-talk.

Okay, I now started talking to my Inner Child often each day. My Inner Child and Adult Being started making decisions together. The Inner Child had to dominate on occasions—how else could I laugh, act silly, do funny things, and be the "character" my grandson loved? But only during these times did my Inner Child take control. My Adult Being made major decisions and helped the Inner Child to grow.

All self-help books claim the wounded Inner Child doesn't have to stay hurt and stuck in the stage in which she was first wounded. With help, love, understanding, and time, she can grow. It's not without struggle and constant daily "talks" with the Adult Being, but she does have the potential to mature. People can become grown-up on the inside as well as the outside, and my hope now was that I could someday fully reach that goal.

CHAPTER 9

Self-Esteem, CoDependency, and Positive Thinking

Even though I had made huge steps in the progression of healing the Inner Child and helping her grow and mature, it seemed an insurmountable task to fully reach this goal of total healing—so big and so far away—and raising my self-esteem seemed sometimes impossible. "I doubt that you need to raise your self-esteem; you seem fine," people would have said had they known I was reading a self-help book. That was farthest from the truth. Remember, I was often a good actress, and my true self-esteem always seemed to have the reflection of the little four-year old girl sitting alone in the corner.

Again, I re-read what Engels had to say on the subject of self-esteem:

- Notice how often you are self-critical (the perfectionist is always self-critical).
- Begin to give yourself more praise.

- Focus on your positive attributes, not on your flaws.
- Work on self-acceptance.
- Set reachable goals.
- Stop taking things so personally.
- Stop letting others define you.
- Stop mind reading.
- Stop comparing yourself with others.
- Stop seeing yourself in all-or-nothing terms.
- Accept that you, and others, are both good and bad.
- Begin nurturing yourself.
- Take care of your body.
- Promote self-healing.

Wow! That was a long list of things that I was asked to do for *me*. Was I worth all of that? By now, I knew that I was.

I knew by now that I needed to work not only on self-esteem but also a topic closely connected to that—my constant seeking of approval from people. I had read a book in the past by Dr. Wayne Dyer entitled *Your Erroneous Zones.* I pulled it off the bookshelf and re-read:

> You may be spending far too many of your present moments in efforts to win the approval of others, or in being concerned with some disapproval that you have encountered. If approval has become a need in your life, then you have some work

to do. You can begin by understanding that approval-seeking is a desire rather than a necessity. Approval-seeking is erroneous when it becomes a need... This need must go! No question marks here. It must be eradicated from you life if you are to gain personal fulfillment.

Again, I reflected on those six days in Europe—those days would not have been tainted if I had not worried about seeking approval from two "friends" who had decided that I was the "third wheel." With the three wheels, I should have become a "tricycle" and gone my own way. I could have dropped them off at the nearest train station (since they were too frightened to drive on the fast-paced European highways), and they could have found their own transportation. However, I knew that I couldn't have been like that, but it was good that the thought was at least now crossing my mind.

It was at this time that my doctor (whom I had gone to see after this incident) said, "Janie, you need to quit being so nice to people." With a smile she added, "You need to develop an attitude." An attitude, huh? My mother used to accuse me of having an attitude...where had it gone? Then the doctor added, "And you know that you didn't lose two friends. You can't lose what you never had." So true... these two ladies had never been friends—hypocrites, bullies, but never friends. So I closed the book on that chapter of my life... something that I couldn't have done a year before. I was growing.

By now, I had also read a great deal on codependency. Yes, I was codependent. All adult children are, and I recognized those traits early in my studying of the adult child of an alcoholic. What is codependency? Engels describes it as well as anyone:

> Children brought up in homes where one or both parents are addicted... become codependent. Growing up in a dysfunctional or addictive family causes a child to feel out of control. Codependent women have very low self-esteem and often feel that their lives aren't worth living.... Only when they are giving to others do they feel worthwhile.... Codependents don't feel happy or content with themselves, so they look outside themselves for happiness.... In their desperate search for love and approval they often seek love from people who are incapable of loving. They worry that people will leave them, and they feel terribly threatened by the loss of anyone they think can provide them with happiness.

Dr. Susan Forward provided a list for codependents in *Toxic Parents*. I could put a mark by almost every phrase:

- Solving his/her problems or relieving his pain is most important to me.
- My good feelings depend on approval from him/her.

- I seldom pay attention to how I feel or what I want.
- I will do anything to avoid getting rejected by him/her.
- I will do anything to avoid making him/her angry at me.
- I am a perfectionist and I blame myself for everything that goes wrong.
- I feel angry, unappreciated, and used.
- I pretend that everything is fine when it isn't.
- The struggle to get him/her to love me dominates my life.

Yes, it all fit my lifestyle, but I was making progress. I was aware of the problems and could begin the long road to recovery.

* * *

It was around this time that I was introduced to a book entitled *The Secret* by Rhonda Byrne. Introduced isn't really the correct word because I believe all things happen because God plans them, and I think that the book was placed directly into my hands by His infinite power (truly, He does not make a mistake). Although I knew many of these concepts from the ideas of Transcendentalism (which I taught when teaching Thoreau to my high school students), it was exactly what I needed to read at that moment.

We are all connected, and we are all One. The

> Great Secret of Life is the law of attraction...
> Thoughts are magnetic, and thoughts have a fre-
> quency. As you think, those thoughts are sent out
> into the Universe, and they magnetically attract
> all *like* things that are on the same frequency.
> Everything sent out returns to the source. And
> that source is You.

Really, I thought? So my positive thoughts attract
more positive thoughts in the Universe, and negativity
attracts negative things? Possibly. I continued on:

> The most important thing for you to know is
> that it is impossible to feel bad and at the same
> time be having good thoughts. That would defy
> the law because your thoughts cause your feel-
> ings....The feeling of love is the highest frequency
> you can emit. The greater the love you feel and
> emit, the greater the power you are harnessing....
> Create your day in advance by thinking the way
> you want it to go and you will create your life
> intentionally....Visualization is the process of cre-
> ating pictures in your mind of yourself enjoying
> what you want. When you visualize, you generate
> powerful thoughts and feelings of having it now.
> The law of attraction then returns that reality to
> you, just as you saw it in your mind.

Okay, it was worth a try. I had read something
similar years before in a self-help book and had tried it
half-heartedly, but at this point in my life, I was willing

to try everything to the fullest. I wanted to heal my Inner Child, live happily on a daily basis, and reach all of my goals.

In fact, *The Secret* also touched on the Inner Child and her healing:

> Treat yourself with love and respect, and you will attract people who show you love and respect…. When you feel bad about yourself, you block the love and instead you attract more people and situations that will continue to make you feel bad about you…. Focus on the qualities you love about yourself and the law of attraction will show you more great things about you….To make a relationship work, focus on what you appreciate about the other person and not your complaints… Laughter attracts hope, releases negativity, and leads to miraculous cures.

One final thought from *The Secret* made me sit up and take notice. It was what I had heard so often before: "Let go of difficulties from your past, cultural codes, and social beliefs. You are the only one who can create the life you deserve."

And then a statement that I read from *Toxic Parents* paralleled what I had just read in *The Secret*: "You are *not* responsible for what was done to you as a defenseless child! You *are* responsible for taking positive steps to do something about it now!"

By that time, I was armed and ready for battle!

❧

CHAPTER 10

On the Road Toward Wholeness

So where am I today? I am still reading, talking to my Inner Child, practicing everything that I've learned the past 35 years about overcoming the pain of being an adult child of an alcoholic, but finally I am doing other things, too. I'm praying often (not just in the morning and at night), trying to enjoy life each day because it could be a person's last (which I always said that I was doing, but was I?), loving my family more, doing things that *I* enjoy, trying to cut down on "work" that doesn't have to be done, and laughing. Yes, laughing. It's an amazing medicine for the soul.

I don't succeed everyday. There are days and even weeks in which I fail miserably. Co-dependency and low self-esteem seem to sky-rocket, and I hit bottom. It's a temporary fall, though, because I have weapons with which to fight now.

My doctor introduced me to Loretta LaRoche's self-help books. *Life Is Not a Stress Rehearsal* and *Life is Short—Wear Your Party Pants* were my first. She is a funny lady and has helped millions to overcome stress in their daily lives.

LaRoche tells a story about her mother, and I'll bet that most of us can identify. Her mother's favorite expression was "you never know." The house would have to be cleaned on Saturdays because "you never know." You'd have to stop in the middle of a wonderful meal to save some leftovers because "you never know." My mother was the same, and it had to do with growing up during WWII and the Depression...you had to save for "that rainy day." However, Loretta wanted some pretty, flowered panties, and her mother continually bought the "hideous" ones that were "sturdy." In a weak moment, her mother bought her some pretty ones, but she had to save them because "you never know." Loretta kept them into adulthood... problem was, they didn't fit anymore.

The anecdote not only displays the absurdity of saving things that we really enjoy for that "rainy day" because eventually they become meaningless for any number of reasons, but it also gives each of us something about which to laugh. Laugher is so good to release toxicity, and doctors say that it actually adds years to a person's life. Don't save things needlessly; I've learned... tomorrow may not come. We need to bring celebration into our daily lives and attempt to find paths of happiness. Again, LaRoche's feelings on the subject of laughter are, "*Celebrate often*! No matter how much stress you might be feeling, pull on those party pants and realize that stress is just another part of the wonderful adventure call *life!*'

Another "mother" story told by LaRoche (maybe her books are truly geared just for me... I love them) brought me to the floor with laughter:

A woman was in the kitchen preparing a roast beef for dinner. Her young daughter was watching her make the meal, and the girl asked, 'Mommy, why did you cut the ends off the roast beef?' And the mother told her: 'Honey, that's just the way you prepare it.' She inquired, 'But why?' And the mother had to think about it for a second and acknowledged, 'You know, I'm not sure why. It's the way my mother did it, and I'm sure she had a good reason.' So she said, 'Let's ask Grandma.' The woman called her mother and asked why she cut the ends off the roast beef. The older woman had to admit that she didn't really know why she did it either, but she did it because that's the way *her* mother prepared a roast beef. So they called the old woman, the child's great-grandmother, who was now in her 90s, and asked her why she cut the ends off the roast beef. 'Well,' the old lady said, 'it's because I didn't have a roasting pan big enough to hold it.'

Aside from laughter, what did I gain from this? I realized that I needed to look beyond what my mother had showed me. I needed to question why I felt abandon-ment, why she chose to deliver the "silent treatment" when I didn't do what she wanted, why she was con-trolling, and most importantly, why she was unable to display love. Of course, it went back to her childhood and the trauma that she must have endured. Must I, however, continue in her tracks? Absolutely not. All of us who are adult children of an alcoholic have a wound-ed Inner Child, are perfectionists, need validation to feel adequate, are super-responsible (or irresponsible), or take life too seriously. We need to laugh, enjoy life each day, and help others who are in the same boat.

For me, writing is a healing process in itself. Putting it all down on paper helps me, but if my writing helps just *one* person through his/her maturing stage, then I've succeeded. Always as a teacher, I felt that if I reached one student that day in the classroom, I could go home feeling successful. That one student might help another and that one still another. The chain reaction would lead to success.

Do I remember any good times with my mother? Yes, from age seven until junior high years, I have incredibly good memories. My mother no longer ob-sessed over my brother's death, and she and I had a mother-daughter friendship. She was able to control me yet, and I didn't mind. I was, of course, a child who needed guidance. She sewed beautiful clothes for me, paid for dance and piano lessons, and attended all of my school functions. Seldom did she utter "I love you," but neither was she ignoring me (except if I didn't do what she wanted), and life seemed "normal."

Are there things that I would like to change if possible? Yes, I'd try harder to talk with my mother. Not accuse, attack, or blame, but just talk. Strangely, I even felt inadequate to just "talk" with her. I didn't know what to say, and I shied away from any kind of intimate conversation. I wish that I would have had the courage to hold her and tell her that I loved her, but again I didn't, and it's too late now. Also, I wish that I could apologize for the additional burdens that I must have placed on her (my anorexia, for example) when she was in a continual precarious state herself. Finally, I wish that I had understood *her* pain and suffering more… I only looked at myself during the time that my healing process first started to take place. I wish I had had the insight to look at my mom's situation and what she had endured. My wounded Inner Child was not mature enough, of course, to do that. Not only was my Inner Child struggling to survive but also my mother's Inner Child must have been in a constant state of chaos. If only I had known and understood at the time.

Have I succeeded in the healing process? No, as I stated earlier, it's a daily struggle. Like an alcoholic, an adult child is never totally healed *forever.* It's an ongoing, arduous task that I (and millions of others) must focus on continually and keep foremost in our minds as we travel life's paths.

The wounded Inner Child is not something I asked for and, of course, has been—at times—a burden. But like all burdens, problems, tribulations, and turmoil, they help sculpt the person into a stronger individual. If we could see and comprehend God's plan, we would understand that all of the concepts that we see as tribulations are really helping us grow. Like soft pliable clay being molded into a beautiful, usable pot, we adult children of an alcoholic with the wounded Inner Child can be formed into God's idea of a person who has overcome mental and physical turbulence of childhood and *survived.*

CHAPTER 11

ॐ

Closer Walk with God

I've always felt that I was a fairly religious person, but trials and tribulations tend to bring a person closer to God. My experience has been that whatever my problem, it seems less serious if I can discuss it with the Lord. He has a way of minimizing what I feel to be huge, and, in addition, He gives me the insight and strength that I need. Indeed, He was in my life when I was a child sitting alone in the living room, and He is still by my side today as I plunder through life with its many problems.

My belief has always been that trials (no matter how awful and turbulent) will make a person stronger in the end. During the time of any chaos, that is a difficult concept to grasp. I have tried to learn to thank God in all circumstances as Paul did. I can remember distinctly thanking Him one day as my husband and I took my mother from the nursing home to the hospital with a broken hip. I thought that I must be insane, but I thanked Him anyway. I don't know what times like that did for my character, but at the least, it made me a more patient person and maybe that was God's sole plan. However, maybe He had a plan in mind for my mother as well.

Often, I have read books by Corrie ten Boom. She was a Dutch Christian who helped hide the Jews in her home during WWII. During one of my visits to Holland, my husband, children, and I sought out her house in Haarlem, Holland. It was a small watch shop with her home in the upper rooms, and we imagined the hundreds of Dutch Jewish people who must have found refuge in the attic rooms during those desperate times of the war.

One story of Corrie has always remained in my mind, and I'll share it now. The Lord had worked miracles (using Corrie) for those around her in the death camp, and He had used both Corrie and her sister, Betsy, to deliver His word to the thousands of Jews who sat with them each night during their secret prayer vigil. After her release from the concentration camp, Corrie made it her quest and goal in life to tell the Word of God to the *world* (literally, she tramped the world with His message). During one of her speeches, she recognized a lady sitting in the audience. She had been the nurse who had been extremely cruel to her sister, Betsy, when she was dying in Ravensbruck Concentration Camp. Corrie described her feelings of "bitterness, almost hatred" that went into her heart at that moment. However, at the very second that she felt hatred, she also knew that she could feel forgiveness because of the Lord. In her book

He Cares, He Comforts, she claimed, "Your love in me is stronger than my hatred and bitterness." And so forgiveness was possible. If Corrie could forgive a Nazi murderer in a concentration camp who preyed upon victims daily, then each of us can forgive people their petty trespasses on a daily basis.

Forgiving is sometimes the easier of the two problems… forgetting is more difficult. Sometimes, I *think* that I've forgotten a problem from my past, and then everything seems to "spring alive" again when an incident reminds me of that past incident. I want to be like Corrie and be able to put everything behind me. That is, of course, easier said than done.

My father taught me to "see the glass as half full, not half empty." I truly try to view my life in that manner. In fact, it is more than half full most of the time, and I'm so thankful for that. Attempting to be positive can often be difficult, but I'm a voracious reader, and self-help books such as *The Secret* have helped me to continue in the path, which I know is good, helpful, and healthy.

All of us have wounds that need healing, and God is the sole healer of all of those wounds. He is the Father who reaches out to give us rest. "Come unto me, all ye that labor and are heavy laden, and I will give you rest"—Matthew 11:28. And so, I end my thoughts with the prospect of "letting go and letting God"… letting go of the past and letting Him heal and lead me forward. I challenge each of you with a wounded Inner Child who are reading this to do the same. It's an ongoing struggle but it's worth it. I continue to cling to a Bible verse in which I firmly believe. "All things work together for good to them that love God"–Romans 8:28.

Works Cited

Bradshaw, John. *The Family.* Florida: Health Communications, Inc. 1988. Print.

Bradshaw, John. *Healing the Shame that Binds You.* Florida: Health Communications, Inc. 1988. Print.

Bradshaw, John. *Home Coming, Reclaiming and Championing Your Inner Child.* USA: Bantum Books. 1992. Print.

Byrne, Rhonda. *The Secret.* New York: Atria Books. 2006. Print.

Dyer, Wayne. *Your Erroneous Zones.* New York: Avon Books. 2001. Print.

Engel, Beverly. *The Emotionally Abused Woman.* New York: Fawcett Columbine. 1990. Print.

Forward, Susan. *Toxic Parents.* USA: Bantum Books. 1990. Print.

LaRoche, Loretta. *Life is Short—Wear Your Party Pants.* California: Hay House. 2004. Print.

Ten Boom, Corrie. *He Cares He Comforts.* New Jersey: Fleming H. Revell Company. 1971. Print.

About the Author

J an Frazier has been in the field of teaching for nearly 40 years, teaching at the secondary level for 25 of those years and taking early retirement in 2002 in order to find time to write. However, as her husband said, "I knew that she'd never leave the field of teaching." She now has been at Bradley University for 12 years, teaching English and Communication.

This is Jan's first attempt at a self-help book, which is based on her life experiences. She is more noted for her young adult adventure/fantasy novels and for her creative nonfiction books, all totaling 18 to date. Jan travels to Europe every year under the guise that she needs more material for her novels since most of her books are set in Europe. She had the honor to take high school students abroad for 15 years and now teaches the January Interim in London for Bradley.

Being named in Who's Who Among America's Teachers on numerous occasions and receiving various awards for her books, Frazier continues to enjoy the creative process of writing plus the rewarding experience of teaching.

See her website: www.janfrazier.com

Books by Jan Frazier

See http://www.janfrazier.com/works.htm
for information concerning all of the books.

STARLIGHT LASER EXPRESS: The Adventures of J.C. VAN WINKLER

GHOST OF A CHANCE: The Adventures of J.C. VAN WINKLER

GLIMPSE OF THE NETHERWORLD: THE Adventures of J.C. VAN WINKLER

DESTINATION DISASTER: A Fight for Life (J.C. van Winkler Series)

THE BELLS OF EUROPE: The Adventures of J.C. VAN WINKLER

THE PATCHWORK QUILT: A Murder Mystery

A MAGICAL CHRISTMAS: The Adventures of J.C. VAN WINKLER

SECRET LAND OF GOJI: The Adventures of J.C. VAN WINKLER

TRANSATLANTIC VOYAGE: The Adventures of J.C. VAN WINKLER

PILGRIMS, INDIANS, SHAKESPEARE, OH MY! The Time Travelers' Saga

BEYOND THE AUSSIES AND ROOS: J.C.'S ADVENTURES IN THE OUTBACK

THE WARMTH OF OPA'S BLANKET

I VISITED EUROPE AND SURVIVED: A Travelogue of Fun and Adventure

TRANSATLANTIC TICKET 1852

EUROPEAN ROOTS AND BEYOND

BORN TO TRAVEL: A European Odyssey

CATCH THE WATERCOLORED WIND: Jamestown 1607 (coming out summer, 2015)

MURDER TIMES THREE

MISSION TO MURDER